GENEALOGY RESEARCH
2018 Edition

How to Organize the Notes, Papers, Documents, Emails, Scans, Computer Files and Photographs for Family Research

GENEALOGY RESEARCH
2018 Edition

**How to Organize the Notes,
Papers, Documents, Emails, Scans,
Computer Files and Photographs for
Family Research**

D. M. Kalten

DMSF

Dedication

This book is dedicated to YOU, the person who would like to preserve the existence and history of your family members.

You are the person willing to take time to put facts together and you deserve credit for your time and efforts.

Table of Contents

Introduction

Designed deliberately as an easy read, the pages in this book will help you get organized with all of your notes, papers, documents, family stories, photographs, computer files and other items that you have, plus as always happens, are still searching for. You will find options for some things and some advice on these pages.

You may have found that a lot of information for your early family members can be found on the web and it is adding to your collection of treasures. You have probably realized that all of your holdings have turned into a confusing mess if you have chosen to read this book.

The thought of 'what should you do to keep organized' may be running thru your mind and you are probably overwhelmed with the feeling of being disorganized. If you feel like you are chasing yourself backwards, then discover you had information you had forgotten about or did not realize you had, you are not alone.

Many who have been doing genealogy research (family research) for a long time has or has had an organization problem and are tired of all the assorted confusions and clutter, both with paper and within their computer. There are usually a lot of photographs to organize and do something with also.

What can you do? The answers are within this book, sometimes with options, as each person has their own personal preferences. Following these pages is your easy way to organization. You may find that you have things you forgot about, or information you did not realize you actually had. Maybe you are wondering how you can organize one document with multi-names on it and keep the information actually with all people that are listed there.

You will find tips on what not to do within this book and those are wise to follow to avoid added work and time as you dig thru all those treasures with information. Organization will help eliminate errors and that organization may show you some missing facts that you had been searching for.

This book is not meant to replace any organization program you may now be working with. It is an aid, one that you may use entirely for a new regime for organization.

Some people already know and use some type of organization habits and/or program. This book is not meant to downplay those. You may though find some help aids here that will really help you. Many people are used to papers, papers, papers with giant paper filing cabinets or boxes of paper confusions. As we move into the digital world, this will help with keeping down the mess while preserving original documents.

There are free programs listed on some pages to help you. I have no connection to any of them other than I use them.

Products mentioned are per my experience. I have no financial ties to them.

The old mess!

Chapter 1 – Simply Put

<u>Do NOT work when you are tired.</u>

- It is extremely easy to error when you are tired. After a long session I often tell myself 'the brain went tilt and it is time to quit for now'.

- It is very easy to try to take shortcuts when tired.

- When tired It is too easy to totally confuse yourself and miss steps or forget something.

- It is very easy to attach a person to the wrong person and suddenly realize one day that you have (examples) a child listed as a parent or a grandchild listed as a sibling to one of the wrong parents or some other strange family situation.

- It is easy to list a birth year after the death year or type the wrong century for one of the years.

<u>ROUTINE</u>:

- This book gives you the basics of what you need to do and puts it in a format to follow. If you choose to change your own routine, that is fine for many things.

- Do NOT miss any steps.

- Make yourself a 'Routine List' that works for you after you understand everything within these pages. Follow 'your' routine to make sure nothing is omitted.

<u>Your OVERALL Goals:</u>

- Organize and file all paper documents.

- Make and Organize genealogy computer files.

- Scan all original documents.

- Scan Photographs, Bible pages, etc.

- Organize email, address and telephone information for all contacts and information.

- Find and retain within your computer every little fact that there is that you currently have.

- Work with a genealogy program.

Chapter 2 – Simple Tools Needed

Trying to get your family paper treasures organized does require a few things, some of which you may already have. Without the proper items it would be like trying to boil water without heat. You will FIRST need to make sure you have these items. I will refer to them as your 'tools' and they are NOT expensive.

It will be assumed that you have a computer, HOWEVER if you do not have a computer just substitute the word 'paper' in place of it where it is applicable throughout these pages.

...

If you do not have a computer, you would be very wise to get one. Some people think they have to learn 'THE computer'. NO, you have to learn some basic, very simple computer basics (like how to turn it on, off, free security programs and keystrokes, otherwise known as typing), and the genealogy program you will use. Your goal is to enter information and save it. The advantage of what you can do with a computer will shock you.

Many people think they do not need a computer as they can access what they need by phone or whatever new electronic gismo comes on the market. This is wrong! Can you picture a large department store keeping track of all their inventory purchases, current inventory, items sold, store sales, refunds, communications with suppliers, trends and payroll without a computer? It would be massive paper work without one.

What You Need – Your Supply List

1: Get at least one CLEAR plastic <u>file</u> tub to start.

These are the stackable type with lids and are available in any office supply or large multi-product store. Try to keep your lid color clear, white or black so that they are a neutral color and if you need to buy more, you can hopefully match them. Watch for a good sale and that does happen often. If funds allow, get what you think you will need keeping in mind the future things you hope to find or order, NOT things found on the web. If you are not using a computer, you will need many more than a person using a computer. How many tubs you will need depends on what you have, what you hope to find and if you will be following every line for both male and female family members. REMEMBER, if you are using a computer, these are for original documents, not scanned or web found items unless you do want to keep paper copies.

DO get at least one extra plastic tub to hold books that may have family mentioned and possible other items that are too large to 'file' in a file folder.

Do NOT get a large metal or wood two or four drawer file cabinet as they are heavy to move, are much heavier when full, are bulky, do rust, can get damaged, are hard to conceal and are not waterproof. The plastic file containers can be stacked or layered in a closet, a basement, an attic or in your work room when you are done with them. You want your work to survive past you so think of the ease of moving and storing the plastic file tubs versus metal or wood file cabinets. If you are limited on space, stacking two or two stacks of two and putting a table cloth over them can actually become an end or coffee table, a table that can be 'show and tell'.

Another advantage with using the plastic tubs is that they can easily be replaced if for some reason one may crack. If you have the wood or metal file cabinets, years of dings, scratches and other abuse can lead to drawers not working correctly and an overall ugly appearance. You cannot easily hide the wood or metal cabinets so they are there to see in whatever room you place them. As far as damage, when you wash the floor or the carpeting, that starts the damage to the metal with rust or with wood it starts the warping and discoloring at the bottom.

2: File Jackets.

These are the manila colored file folders that all offices use. Get the standard size, not legal size. Legal size will not be needed often, if at all, and you <u>do</u> want the folders to fit in your file containers and filed, not lying in the bottom under regular sized folders. For legal size papers, you will have to fold them.
OPTION: You can use one plastic tub for larger manila folders and papers. This will however, result in more than one file for 'that' person as most will be in the normal size folders.

DO get the STRAIGHT EDGE, open sides, file folders. These have no tabs and the sides are not sealed. The divided tab folders will not mean a thing when you start adding in more people alphabetically. In fact, the tabs cause confusions. The straight edge also gives you enough writing room. You want the standard ones, not ones that expand. Over time, you can always invest in expandable ones if needed for a person and remember they come in varied expandable sizes. The expandable ones are closed on the sides. Should you need more than one folder for one person and do not have any expandable folders, you can do 'Folder 1 of X' in pencil on the far right of the label, but in this case, expandable does work better for organization. With the expandable folders, you can set the other folders inside of them. That may help when you have a person with multiple folders due to a lot of information and documents being found.

Do NOT get the colored file folders thinking that you are going to color code family lines. It does not work. Each generation doubles family groups and adds in new surnames considering the female lines. By the time you get to just a few generations back you will be out of color options to buy and how would you color code their children? Folders do not come in multi-color options. Do not drive yourself crazy with expensive color file jackets or try any other color coding with paper files. You can rely on name and dates for your file organization. Your genealogy program will come into play with keeping track of family lines. The goal with these folders is organizing papers, <u>not</u> sorting your family lines.

The ONLY time any color coding of a file jacket may help you is if you want to keep track of people that came from the heritage of your father or your mother. With that, you will use only two colors and it is best to use a felt color pen or marker on a corner of the folder label due to the price of colored folders. Obvious colors to use for that would be pink and blue ink but pink is rather hard to read. An option would be to use black ink and then with a color marker, draw thru the text on your label using pink or blue.

If you are lucky enough to go back hundreds of years with one of your lines, that is a lot of color coding (a lot of files). Your parents would be the first folders to color code for that. You do NOT color code yourself a single color. You can color yourself pink and blue, or possibly you may want to make yourself green for 'go' (where <u>you</u> are starting). Your children do not get a color code. Keep in mind that the manila folders are for original documents unless you do want a printed copy of what is easily found on the web and should be in your computer.

3: Mechanical Pencils.

Mechanical pencils are available in varied brands but the cheap ones can be very hard to read due to the nature of the pencil lead they use. Look for Paper-Mate Sharp Writer #2 USA that come in a deep yellow color. They are not expensive. I have seen them at all office supply stores, drug stores and dollar classed type stores. Keep one near you and remember that a pen can be your worst enemy. These keep a nice sharp writing tip where a normal pencil does not.

4: Sharpies.

You want at least one Extra Fine and one Wide Sharpie permanent ink pen in the color of black.

5: Yellow self-stick papers
 (Often called 'stickies' and sticky note sheets).

Get some yellow self-stick paper tablets. There are varied brands at a variety of prices. A size around 2" to 3" or 2" x 4" square is usually sufficient. This may be needed to add a note onto a paper original or whatever little need you may run across. When using these, do NOT put any sticky area against any print on a document.

6: Genealogy Computer Program.

You should have a computer and a genealogy computer program in this modern day. It will greatly open up what you can do and what you can find. You will be able to put your information down quickly in a readable sense for your family connections. Learning that program is your main learning curve. Most are fairly easy to master, at least with the basics of the name, dates of birth, marriage, spouse, children, death.

7: Computer program Word or equivalent.

You will need the Microsoft program known as Word, a word processing program, or a program equal to it. If you do not have Word, there are free programs you can download that do the same things. You will have many uses for this type of program beyond working with genealogy research.

8: Back Ups.

If you are using a computer, you should have an external drive, thumb drives or some other means of doing backups. You DO want to be able to do backups for your genealogy work, that including your genealogy entries into a program, all photographs and documents that you will hold in your computer.

If you choose to pay for an on-line back-up service, that is your choice. However, also do back-ups that you can physically get to. I myself also send a backup of my genealogy program entries to an off-site email address I have. If you should do that, such as a Yahoo email address, make sure you know how often you DO need to actually enter that site as many sites will delete everything if the account is not accessed every so often, possibly every three months.

A free and easy program to download for backups is Karen's Replicator. You can set it to backup just your genealogy work and whatever else you chose. You can set it to automatically back up your entire computer or whatever parts you want. An advantage to this program is that you can open your backup and it is just like looking at your computer file folder. You can open a file there and copy from it which is an advantage. It makes it very easy to carry your 'genealogy folder' with you on a thumb drive to view or share (copy and paste) photographs and documents. Think of this program for dual uses. Karen's Replicator will automatically backup files, directories, even entire drives! Karen's Replicator copies selected files from one drive/folder to another.

Karen, the lady who designed the replicator program has passed away. You can find the FREE program (Karen's Replicator 3.6.9) at archive.org with download still available https://archive.org/details/ptreplicator-setup On the page that opens, there are three download options on the right.

On any backup, it should be dated. Depending on what you choose, consider using the following format unless the backup you do does dating automatically. Date and backup name example: 2017 01 01 BU gen (year, month, day, backup, genealogy).

WARNING: Check your computer to make sure it will backup levels of files. You may have to drag deep files to your desktop to get them to backup. For instance: You may have to drag THE large People folder file to the desktop, then drag it back to where it belongs after a backup.

9: Vinyl Paper Holders.

This is an option for special original documents such as a very old original birth certificate that has been handed down to you or one you had to pay big bucks for at a county health department. You may want to find clear plastic sleeves in ARCHIVAL quality for those very special things. There are a variety of brands and they can be found in various office supply stores. Most tend to be made for three ring notebooks but you can find them without that feature. The edge can be cut off of the three ring folders or just leave it on. These will be filed in the previously mentioned manila folders. It is a good idea to have at least one box of these at hand. The size holds up to 8 1/2” x 11” papers. There are varied manufacturers so do some comparisons as you want the less expensive, non-busy type, but archival.

For larger paper items you can get large hard plastic holders at some hobby type shops, possibly by special order for specific sizes, and those can be filed in a tub for oversized items. I have purchased those from a baseball hobby shop for very old maps in varied sizes.

10: Paper.

Get a pad of paper with lines on it. Not loose paper, but a pad. This is for running notes of things you will think of that you want or need to do. You will find yourself filing a paper away or maybe doing dishes when you think of something you want to do or need to do. WRITE it down as it is very easy to totally forget something very important. You will have a running list, not a page for each thought or person. This is for use even after you are organized. Cross things off as an item is done.

11: The last things you will need are time, patience and a routine with your steps.

Time to work on your organization and the patience to do it is a big key to getting organized. A routine with your genealogy habits will keep you organized. Never put off a step with what you are doing in the organization category if you want to stay organized. This IS very important.

It is impossible to get organized overnight. It will take some time. The time it will take to get totally organized depends on how many paper and photo treasures you have accumulated. Set your mind to the fact that you are going to start at one spot and not deviate from it, even if you can only work a few hours a week on it. An example of not deviating from something: Let's say you have a box of documents that you want to sort out. You are going to make a computer folder for each main person shown on the document and one for the actual document to file in the main persons manila folder. You get to the second document and it triggers questions you have. Don't head to the internet. Head for a yellow sticky, make your notes concerning what you want to do and put it on the folder or use your notepad.

If you have an area of the house where you can leave things out after working on it for a while do so. It helps you stay organized with what you are doing and will allow you to slip in an hour or so of work when you have extra time. It's really hard to organize things when you have to keep gathering things up and hide them. Adding some caution here: If you have pets, try to keep them out of that area when you are not there. If all else fails, put a table cloth or sheet over it. Cats love to lay on what you are doing and manage to scatter things.

<u>To sum up this 'tools' section</u>, your first steps, here are your first priorities:

Go shopping and get what you need from the previous list.

Figure out what area of the house you are going to work in. Clear out any clutter there and get it ready for you to work in.

Gather your paper documents and various paper treasures.

Set up your TV and/or radio along with hopefully a side table for your pop or coffee. Keep all liquids away from your papers.

DO finish reading these pages if you have not done so.

Chapter 3 – Where to Begin with Papers

After you do have your supplies and your work area set up, hopefully with a large table area, you are ready to start organizing all of your paper documents.

As many businesses are now doing, your goal is not to have a paper mess, but to be a somewhat paperless operation. Original documents you do want to keep.

Keep in mind that the manila folders are for only paper documents you have in your possession that are originals or copies of originals that you cannot replace. This is NOT for documents you can find on the web or for documents emailed to you unless you have a reason for wanting a paper printed copy. More concerning computer gained items will follow. If you do NOT have a computer, you will be filing all that you do have in these folders. One folder means one person, not one document.

This is not for coloring coding family lines or for anything else except for filing away original documents in an organized manner. You are currently getting yourself organized to do 'the genealogy work' later. More on this is on later pages.

...

<u>First</u>

You are going to start with just one plastic file tub. If you have bought more than one tub, put the others out of the way until you need another. Get that part of the clutter out of your way or you can use them to help divide papers if you chose to do some sorting first. Presorting is not necessary unless you want to see what you have. That is your choice.

<u>Second</u>

Grab two (or four) pieces of printer or copy machine paper and that WIDE black Sharpie pen. On each paper mark it in BIG lettering 'ORIGINALS – *Do NOT Destroy*' '*Genealogy Documents*' '*A – Z*' doing so in three lines and without the quote marks. The first line you may want to underline in red, possibly even using a yellow highlight marker thru those words may be a good idea. These will be your tub labels to fasten on the <u>inside</u> of either two or four sides of each tub. This is your warning to family. Set something of no value under the paper when you do the writing as the ink may bleed through onto your table. The A - Z lettering is for referencing the surname only.

Put each paper into a clear vinyl paper holder (on the tool list under 'Optional') and tape it with the words facing outwards on each side on the INSIDE of the tub. This keeps your tub labels from being bent, torn and from getting dirty as files are entered, removed, refiled and tub movements. Use two pieces of scotch tape or clear packaging tape at the top of each to hold each in place. You may choose to start with just one label (not two or four) for now.

As you add a file tub for more paper items, change your paper labeling to fit the holdings. The first file tub may soon be 'Genealogy Documents A-N'. Change your labels as you add file tubs with holdings. Over time as you fill your tub/s you can add paper or thin cardboard dividers between each first letter of files such as between surnames that begin with A and those that begin with B, labeling each with A or B, and so on. Should you eventually have many tubs and they may contain many surnames beginning with S. You can do dividers between those 'S' surnames and also note the variations on your tub labels such as SA - SM and SO - SZ.

If you have a tub where the folders you are entering are falling down, which will happen when you begin a tub, add a small empty box to the back until it is not needed any further. That also adds a nice place to hold your pens, pencils, yellow sticky paper pads and any other items you may find of use.

Third

Get your first blank manila file folder and grab a document. The first paper on the top of the stack is fine. You are going to do your first manila folder for people, not for each document!

With your THIN tip black Sharpie pen you are going to label the straight edge manila folder. You want the last name, first name, middle name or initial, year of birth, and year of death on it starting at the far left. Your folder label will read (example) *SMITH Susannah A. 1875-1952* with no period, no quotes, and no other excess markings.

You can add a note following the name and dates IN PENCIL now or later. Leave space between your main label and your added note. Three examples of a full folder heading with a pencil note follow. Each would be a single line across the top of the folder.

Example 1: *SMITH Susannah A. 1875-1952 Daughter to SMITH John & JONES Mary*

Example 2: *SMITH Susannah A. 1875-1952 marriages 3: BROWN – SMITH – BING*

Example 3: *SMITH Susannah A. 1875-1952 Maryland research*

Again, you are NOT doing folders per document. You are doing folders per person. ALL documents for that person will go into that file folder. Remember you are currently just organizing, NOT doing research. It is very easy to get side tracked and head to doing more research for a person. For now, make a note on your pad of paper if you have a thought about doing something concerning someone.

If more than one person is on a document, label and file it under the MAIN person. If a marriage document, that would be the man. You can do multi copies in your computer but more on that later.

NOTE: Females are listed and filed under their BIRTH name with genealogy research. This is also true for the manila folders and also in a genealogy program with their entry. Your pencil note on the right side of the folder tab can be *'Married to XXXX, Year'*. Use pencil as notes on the right of a label can often need changed and the pencil markings make it easy to do without leaving a crossed out ink mess.

Fourth

Put the folder into your file tub. You have just made and filed your first physical person folder of documents. Begin with your second folder and person. When or if you come across another document for a person where you have already made a folder, just add the document to that folder. Remember, you are not doing research right now.

Always make sure you do not have a name folder already started for a person with each new document. No matter what type of document you have in your hand, it will go into the person's folder (manila folder) unless it is too large such as a book. In that case, add it to a tub for oversized items and start a list to set in that tub for the contents of it. Also, make a note in or on the manila folder.

Fifth

Continue until you have ALL of your original papers into manila folders and into the file tub/s. If you have a lot of papers and you do not think you will ever get done with folders, keep telling yourself that once they are done you will know what you have and where it is, or rather, which way is up concerning your paper mess!

Should you come across a document that you want to add a note to, grab those yellow sticky papers mentioned in 'tools'. Write on the sticky, not on the original. Putting a sticky directly on an original can over time lift the ink off the original so use caution where you place it.

If you are entering the document into an archival clear folder first, then write on the BACK side of the yellow sticky. Attach that to the INSIDE front of the plastic holder. The handwriting will face you, will be protected and will not be attached to the original. If you have a white band on the archival folder for a notebook (the area where holes are for notebook insertion), you can cut that off first, if wanted.

When you have all of the papers filed away in your file tub/s, knowing that they are filed in a protected, organized manner for the person they pertain to, you are ready to head to the computer. Your next goal is to scan the original documents but <u>do NOT do so until you read the section concerning the people folders for the computer</u>. Make sure you do not forget that the scans need to be done.

At this point, when you have everything into the plastic tubs, you should feel pretty good with your accomplishment!

Chapter 4 - Organizing Your Computer

All of your original documents that you physically hold should now be filed away in the labeled manila folders and sitting in the plastic file tub/s. Put the lid on them as we will get back to these later because you do have to scan them. You will do those paper file scans after you understand the folders that you have to make in your computer.

This chapter will start the building of 'people files' for EVERYONE that you do have any information for. These computer 'people files' will hold EVERYTHING you have for a person, that including things found on the web, anything emailed about a person, and scans you will do of your original documents. It will also hold any family stories and miscellaneous notes you may have for a person. The notes and stories will be in a Word.doc or similar program (documents noted earlier).

You can also begin a file named for a last name only, such as for scanned pages from a book or books that mentions many people in a family surname line. Perhaps you have city or county information you want to save. You can begin a folder that says (example #1) *SMITH Book Pennsylvania pub 1901* and (example #2)

BOOK Ohio Montgomery Co Dayton city history (no periods or commas). You can adjust those last words anyway you want such as 'CITY HISTORY' in place of 'city history'.

You DO also want to see the section on photographs. Photographs are the LAST thing to deal with.

...

This next step in getting organized is to organize all the treasures for your family research that you have in your computer. You are now going to start a file in the computer for each person you have information on within the computer. You will come across things that you may want to check out on the web. DON'T. Later! Make a note on that pad of paper. Remember, you are organizing, not currently doing researching.

FIRST (Folder 1- Main level)

You DO need to begin with one main folder that says 'Genealogy Work', (or) 'Family Research', (or) 'Genealogy ALL HERE' or whatever title is comfortable for you (without the quotes).   Place that folder on your main desktop screen or in My Documents. It is easiest to work with if you put it on your main screen. You can always drag this main genealogy folder to a different location if you change your mind where you want it. I myself prefer it on my main screen as it is less work for me to find the folder.

If you do not know how to make a folder in your computer follow this: On your main screen you right click, then left click on 'New', and then left click on 'Folder'. Your folder will be yellow in color. The folder titled 'New Folder' will show on your main screen. Go to that folder that says 'New Folder' and it should allow you to change the name. If it does not, do a right click, then a left click on 'Rename'. Enter the folder name. Click on the Enter key.

Your main genealogy folder (level #1)
This is a yellow folder on your main computer screen.

The goal is to get everything you have concerning your family research into this first computer file with subfolders (different levels of folders). This includes the original documents you have that should be scanned to the computer. What you will be doing is really no different than paper filing, only this is digital.

One advantage of having something in your computer is that if you want to check something or give a copy to someone, it should be ready to view, to print or to email to another from these files. Once scanning is done for an original document, your <u>original</u> paper item should be filed away in the plastic file tubs and you will have no research reason to get them out. If you want to view an item, open it on your computer where you can enlarge it for viewing if necessary. Viewing on screen after scanning allows you to alter an item lighter, darker or clearer, if needed. You can also save that alteration.

Some people try to save all similar documents, such as birth certificates, in one folder. To clarify, some people may try to keep hundreds of birth certificates in one folder. DO NOT do this. Keep everything for one person with the person.

Following is how to file things within your computer to totally stay organized with all of your treasures. The goal is that you are going to do people folders, the same as you did for paper documents in your plastic tubs, only digital.

SECOND (Folder 2 – Second level)

Begin a subfolder in the main genealogy folder, the one you just made. You open the main genealogy folder (level #1), click on your screen within the folder and do the same as you did to make folder #1.

Name it 'People Researched', 'Family Found', 'Family Research – PEOPLE', 'People Files' or whatever name lets you know that each person you have researched or have information for is in this subfolder. I will call this subfolder #2a. As you get familiar with the folders, you can always rename them to suit yourself. I call this folder in my computer my people files.

With Folder #1 open and Folder 2a closed, do a second folder within Folder 1. This is a second subfolder that should be named 'Genealogy Overflow' which I will call subfolder #2b. This will sit side by side with 'Family Research - People' or whatever name you chose to hold the people.

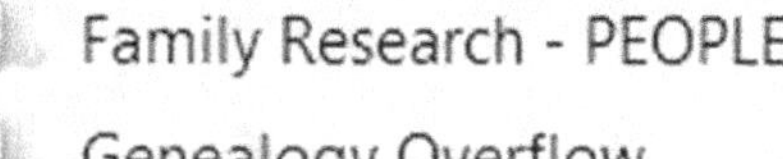

The above is IN the main folder (level #1)
being level #2 (folder 2a and 2b).

When opening the main genealogy folder (level 1), the above is what you should now see (level #2).

To Clarify:

LEVEL ONE = Main Genealogy Folder

LEVEL TWO =
Folder 2a = Family Research – PEOPLE
Folder 2b = Genealogy Overflow

The 'Genealogy Overflow' folder (folder 2b) will hold varied types of miscellaneous items and you can do subfolders within it. This can be state information, maps, links or whatever you need. Let's say you have done a lot of research for Cincinnati in Hamilton County, Ohio and have things you want to save for further searches or references. Here you would make a folder saying 'OHIO Hamilton Co' (no quotes). Anything you come across for that county history, maps for it, links for it saved in a Word Document, and other varied miscellaneous items should be placed in that folder if it is something you want to keep. This is not people. It is area help aids and information.

To give you an example of things to keep in your Genealogy Overflow folder, you may find the full city directories on line for a city and you want to keep downloads of the books. You then, in the Genealogy Overflow folder, make a sub-folder under the state and then under a folder for the county that says City Directories, also naming the place and put those directory downloads there. A somewhat visual of your folders would be: *Genealogy ALL HERE > Genealogy Overflow > Ohio > County Hamilton > City Directories*. Counting the main folder ('Genealogy ALL HERE, level

1') you would be FIVE levels deep. Can you see how simple it would be to get to exactly what you want among possibly thousands of files you may end up having? If you are wondering why 'County Hamilton' was used instead of 'Hamilton County', it is so that all the counties in Ohio show together and automatically sort alphabetically.

You can also do subfolders at deeper levels in your People Folders.

You can add and rearrange whatever you want in 'Genealogy Overflow' other than people. Keep the people in the People folder, folder #2a.

Following is a partial view of my 'Genealogy Overflow' folder which is general information, not information for any direct person. For instance, in the 'Census' folder I have a word document that lists the enumeration dates for all past U.S. census years, another for web links and more, all concerning both Federal and State census years, those being divided by two sub-folders to reflect a federal or a state census. In the Military and Wars folder I have every war listed in subfolders, each holding a lot of information.

In my Genealogy Overflow folder I actually have hundreds of folders. Shown is a small sample. The dot (.) prior to all wording tells me I have sorted and correctly named everything in that folder to allow all to fall alphabetically in correct categories for the subfolder titles each holds.

To further explain the Genealogy Overflow folder (level #2) envision this: I am walking into a library (main genealogy folder, level #1). I want to go to the area in the library for wars (genealogy overflow, level #2). I want to go to a specific war (level #3 for war choice).

A small sample of my 'Genealogy Overflow' folder follows.

. Books

. Cemetery - Headstones

. CENSUS

. Countries other than US

. Deaths

. FBI The (Genealogy)

. George Washingtons Journal 1754

. Google How to Search

. Illnesses & Diseases

. Immigration

. Maps & Links

. Military & Wars

. Money Early

. Names

. Occupations

. Photos varied info

. Quakers

Following is an example of what I have in the federal census folder. It is a Word document stating the enumeration dates for each census with each showing a sentence for each census. These are ready to copy to a summary for any person. Note I do need to adjust the 'questioned on date' for each.

'The 1790 Census: The 1st US Federal Census, all information was to reflect the status of each question as of 2 Aug. The family was questioned on XXXX.' Note: You fill in the date per family.

THIRD (Folder 3 – Third level)
In the PEOPLE FOLDERS:

With the PEOPLE folder open (folder #2a) do a series of folders that say 'A birth names' thru 'Z birth names' without quotes. This will be a folder for every letter of the alphabet. You can make these as you find people or get them all ready now.

A partial view of level #3 with the letter 'U' not added follows:

    Q birth names
    R birth names
    S birth names
    T birth names
    V birth names
    W birth names

Level #3 in the PEOPLE folders – SURNAMES.

Level #1: Main genealogy folder (folder #1).
Level #2: Family Research – People (folder #2a).

Level #3: A to Z birth name files.
(Within folder #2a)

If you have 100 people all born with a last name beginning with an 'S', they will all be placed in the 'S birth names' folder in further subfolders. This is no different than going to a filing cabinet for genealogy and going to the drawer for S, then searching for the correct last name.

Fourth (Folder level #4)

This is sub-folders to the above A to Z last name sub-folders. AS you begin to add folders for people, first add a folder that says the last name and the words 'birth names' under the appropriate first letter of the surname. Example: I am one who has SMITH as a research name. So opening the previous 'S birth names' folder (level #3), I want to add a folder within it (level #4) that says 'SMITH birth names'. This is where I will find THE PEOPLE BORN as a SMITH.

   SMIT birth name
   SMITH birth name

The previous view shows level #4, a partial view in my 'S birth names' folder.

An example of how this falls into folders is:

Genealogy ALL HERE >
Family Research – PEOPLE >
S birth names >
SMITH birth name.

This is no different than looking in a file drawer
marked 'S' and looking for SMITH.

Fifth (Folder level #5)

This IS your people. Here is where you want folders
for the individual people. This is within your birth
name folders. So if you are in that SMITH file drawer,
now you are searching for (needing) a first name.

You will be making files within the Last Name files for
individual people. Each should be named to show last
name, first name, middle name or initial, then
hopefully birth year and the death year. If birth and
death are not known, add what best quickly describes
a person.

The following example shows a partial view of the file
contents of my 'SMITH birth name' folder shown in
previous level #4 view. The labels reflect what is best
known about each person. These people are actually
seven different lines in my family, not all from one
lineage.

SMITH Hanna HAMILTON FELIX McKEEVER

SMITH Isaac ca 1787- born PA

SMITH Isaac ca 1801-

SMITH James ca 1800 Ireland-

SMITH Jane Lacey 1813-1897

SMITH John W or I.J.orW. ca 1816- born OH

SMITH Margaret ca 1831- born OH

SMITH Margaret E ca 1847 - born OH

SMITH Martha ca 1845- born OH

SMITH Mary Inez AMONS - GUILD - LUCAS 1834-1907 born OH

SMITH Mathias ca 1801Germany-

SMITH Nathaniel ca 1798 NJ-

Above, level 5 is THE people.

Note: If you list the 'ca' after the year, if the year is an approximate year, it can alter the sort with same first names.

The goal: You want to file everything for each person under that person's name folder. For example a file named 'SMITH John 1825-1900' should hold everything you have for <u>that</u> John SMITH. If there are eight John Smiths you would have eight folders with each further identified in the folder title as best as you have information for. The birth and death are the best if you know those dates. If you need to use the 'ca' in a date, you need to add it after the year so all years line up in sequence. My example above is opposite of that. If you have information and you are not sure of exactly which (example) John SMITH it goes to, make a 'SMITH John in question' folder.

SMITH John 1724ca-1724ca bro to John b 1725ca

SMITH John 1725ca-1810ca

SMITH John 1750ca-1848

SMITH John 1775ca-1842

SMITH John 1800ca-1876

SMITH John 1825-1900

SMITH John 1852-1928

SMITH John 1886-1970

Above is another example of level #5 folders. This showing one name, multi people, some with 'ca' dates with the 'ca' noted <u>after</u> the dates.

If you wonder why I made the 'bro' note in the first name above, it is because often when a child died, the next born was given the same name. It is an aid to me.

Try not to get to wordy in your titles as it can interfere with the ability to make further sub-folders under people's names.

To begin with making your first actual person name folder, begin a folder for a name of someone you have in your computer and move whatever may be scattered around in your computer for that person TO that file. The easiest way to do that is to have two windows open, one is for searching and the other one showing the persons folder. Then drag item/s over to it. Just be careful of where you are dragging to and do not work on this if you are tired. It helps to open that person folder and then drag to it. You can also cut and paste, or copy, paste and delete the first one.

IF the item you drag to a folder mentions MORE than one person, make a folder for EACH person named in the item. Then go to where the item is, click on 'copy' and then paste a copy into each person folder who secondly was named.

You may have to use your search feature for your computer to find things that you may have if you have a mess. If you use that feature, remember with each new search for the same name will bring up things you just moved.

Do this across the board and get your computer organized. Do not go any further with anything until you have your computer organized with those folder names with all people gathered and put where they belong. If you are holding documents and information on 100 or 10,000 people, for whomever you have a find for, they need a folder even if it is just to hold a Word Document note.

As you get the people folders made, you will see organization building. Do NOT at this time try to organize the contents put into those people folders. You can do that later as you work on a person as explained further in this book. Right now your goal is to get the computer organized with folders and not to be sidetracked from that end of the organization project. Make notes on your pad if need be for a thought on someone or something.

Once in a while, restart your computer. It helps 'set' things on your computer.

Along the way with building your files, you may want to use the FREE program (a fast download) that is named CCleaner (https://www.piriform.com/ccleaner) to get rid of a lot of junk like old memory things and various other things that clog up computers. It has various options, one being a junk cleaner and another being a registry cleaner. IF you are afraid to clean the registry, ignore that part but do use the basic cleaner. It is all mainly old memory things that will be cleaned out that you really do not want. Restart your computer prior to using this.

You will also have to do 'defrags' (defragmentation) since you will be moving a lot of information. Again I stick with the same company and use their FREE defrag program at https://www.piriform.com/defraggler.

Do not try to put all documents into one mass holding under a document title such as census records. To put it another way, if you have 500 different census records, do not put them all under one file titled census records. You will drive yourself crazy with finding a specific record, if you can remember you have it. Keep everything under a person's name.

For census items, you can do a copy and paste for each person named on a census which in turn helps you build a people file for those people in your computer. The census will give you a 'ca' birth date.

A tip on naming a census find, no matter what family member it is for, title your census label in the following manner, (example) '1930 Census SMITH John HOH 1875-1951' (with no quotes). The 'HOH' means who the head of the household is. The years are his birth and death, if you already know those dates. The advantage of listing the year first is that it will automatically file in sequence to other events and years in the People Folder.

If you have a census that has say seven family members noted, copy it to all other six people folders. That copy in each person's folder is ready for when you are ready to research each person and eventually do a final summary for a person, that being discussed further in this book.

Sixth (Folder Level #6)

You may have original old Bible entries, a baptism record, a hand wrote very old letter, military papers, census finds, emails from someone giving you information and many other items for a person. Each should be held in a folder named as such under that person's NAME FOLDER (Person Folder). You therefore have a MAIN NAME folder (preceding folder #5) with now a Sixth Level of subfolders, those being the items FOR an individual person. You can do this level of organization later when you actually work on the genealogy for this person.

OPTION: If you would not want this level of folders for everything and just want the information there to sort thru, that is your choice. Where folders come in handy is to (1) keep all according to dates if some is in a level #6 folder, (2) keep multi items for one event together.

The following is a small, partial view of subfolders for a person born as **SMITH Mary**.

- . 1872 Cinn city dir GUILD widow
- . 1873 city dir
- . 1880 Census LUCAS John B HOH
- . 1881 Oct 13 Did Mortgage to LEIGHTON
- . 1884 Note by Lee (TAYLOR) Middleton
- . 1900 Census LUCAS John B HOH
- . 1903 Cutter St incident
- . 1905 Cutter St resident
- . 1907 SMITH, Mary I death +

Proceeding is examples of level 6 folders for one person. Each holds THE information as described in the folder label. Some hold multi home photos and various notes. The dot '.' before each one tells me I have sorted and correctly named everything in that folder.

To put the folder levels into a closer context, here is the folder ladder:

Level 1- Genealogy ALL HERE >
I am walking into the library.

Level 2a - Family Research - PEOPLE (and 2b-Genealogy Overflow) >
I am in the library and I have two direction choices. I chose PEOPLE, not the area information.

Level 3- (under folder 2a) A-Z birth names >
I find the shelf for all the surnames. I am going to go to the S surnames.

Level 4- Surname birth names > (Such as SMITH birth names. Not first names.)
I find the SMITH birth names.

Level 5- PEOPLE In the appropriate surname folder (SMITH Mary file is here) > (Last name, first name, birth & death years on label.)
I go to THE person I want.

Level 6- Contents for each person (the content folders for SMITH Mary are here).
I am in the person file and I am looking at all of my choices for THAT person.

Following the preceding organization will surprise you
with how easy it will be to find who you want and what
you want.

There are a lot of varied genealogy programs on the market. Each promotes themselves as the best, of course. I have researched them all and tried most.

Some people actually use two or more genealogy programs due to what one may do and the other will not do. Some people try to keep each totally current with the use of GEDCOMs, an outdated item many now say. The problem with GEDCOMs is that it only transfers certain information and far from all that can be entered into a program. For safety sake, currently think of a GEDCOM as name, birth, death, and the marriage dates only. The history of GEDCOM can be found on the web if you are not familiar with the term or what it is.

Some programs offer more space than others for the entry of information. Some programs offer a few bells and whistles others do not. I've never heard anyone say they like their program 100%. The key is to pick one that allows you to do as much as possible and then YOU choose what you want to use with the program.

To compare or pick a genealogy program, there are comparison charts on the web. Knowing when those sites are updated is important as programs are changing, some are gone and new ones will be available. Research each in depth as you do not want to change to a different program after entering hundreds or thousands of people into the one you first use. The thought of rechecking all those files for missing information on some type of a transfer between programs is daunting.

To start, at this point with your 'ORGANIZATION', with whatever program you are using, only enter the name, birth &/or baptism, marriage, and death under the correct parents. Although it is very tempting to add all types of information, don't do it now. Make notes in a Word.doc (to file in your 'Summaries' – to be discussed further in this book) or make notes on your pad of paper.

It is a good idea to get into the habit of entering a person into your genealogy program right after you get the 'People Folder' made in your computer files.

Second Reminder: Make sure you <u>DO</u> enter the people under the correct parents if the parents are known. It's amazing how many works I have seen where a grandparent or parent is shown as a child to the children, no matter the birth being prior to the children being born.

Right now what you are concerned with is organizing and you will be building files IN your computer and in a genealogy program, not entering details other than the identifiers (name, birth, baptism, marriage, death) in the genealogy program.

Do not get side tracked. Further in this book there is more information concerning entering more information that can be found on a document.

I am an avid TMG (the Master Genealogist) user and I cannot at this time make a recommendation for another program. My old TMG program works even though it is off of the market. Until things settle in the future with other makers, I'll keep using it. Currently there is nothing that can take the transfer of all the varied types of information I have entered into it and those do not allow a place to type it in. It is said there is the HRE program coming out. This will be a replacement for the TMG program which was known as the Cadillac of programs. It is unknown when it will be available. Information for this can be found at

https://historyresearchenvironment.org/hre-for-users-of-the-master-genealogist/.

Recently, another major genealogy program company has announced it will be discontinuing its genealogy software program. They are trying to get everyone to enter things on their site, on the web for a MONTHLY fee. A sad fact is, as some companies do and will be charging for viewing, all your work puts gains into their bank account, not yours. There is also the thought of **how** do you access your work or make changes to your own work if you are not a paid member.

Recently I entered information for a dozen people into three different genealogy programs to test them. Two were horrible in my estimation and the third is catching up to those in the back line. That is where I am glad I have my people files and SUMMARIES (discussed further in this book).

If you use a program that puts your information on line as you type it, be sure to read their terms first. A very well-known company appears to have all the rights to do what they want, including selling your genealogy information, even though they say you own the information.

With any on line program you must decide if you want your work to be that open to the world which entices others to copy it without doing their own research. Anyone a little bit experienced can soon see how spelling errors are copied over and over among different people, that showing that those people do not do their own research.

All things considered right now, entering only the name, birth, baptism, marriage and death into your genealogy program is sufficient – other than entering them under the correct parents.

Chapter 6 – Entering Manila Folder Holdings

If you have the People Folders made for everyone you have information for within your computer, at this point, you can begin entering what you have in your manila folders into the computer. This is everything that is in the manila folders.

You now scan the papers to the People folders. Note: You can opt to do this after the manila folders are organized, prior to organizing the information in your computer, using those manila folder files to start your People files.

You may find that you do need to make more People folders for people. If you have begun the basic information into a genealogy program, be sure to add the people after you get their People folder made IF they have not yet been entered, per your computer organization. Reminder: For now, this is full name and the birth-death dates only.

All scanners are a little different but the basics are the same. Most people scan with normal resolution at normal (100%) size in black and white for papers and documents. IF the document has any dirt or spots on it, it will look like black blobs. Those 'blobs' can interfere with reading ability. <u>I suggest you scan all documents in color, seriously</u>. You can always choose black and white for printing, for any needed print you may do. The scan in color makes the document a true reproduction and there would be no question as to what word may be under a black blob or a dark area on the original.

Most people save their scans as a JPEG/JPG. There are other options, some types taking a lot of hard drive space. If you chose the larger formats for saving all documents and photographs, that can be a detriment with backups if you have hundreds or thousands of giant files. To upload a photo to a website or into a report, a JPEG/JPG will work fine.

To save a scan in varied formats, you need to scan it just once. Keep the photo on screen from your scanner to do various saves.

If more than one person is named on a document, scan it once, save it to the People file for the main person mentioned and then copy and paste it to folders for the other people named.

If you wonder why you are saving multiple copies of something, the answer is that you want all of your people files complete for each person. It also saves you a lot of time hunting elsewhere for something IF you can remember that the person is mentioned on that document. This will make more sense when you read the chapter on summaries.

If you have old letters from family members, those should be treated as documents and definitely scanned. It should have a copy in the People folder for who wrote the letter and copies in the folders for any people mentioned in it.

After you have all of your manila folders scanned into your computer, it is time to find the place to put your plastic tubs. You will not need these again unless you have additional documents to file. Your documents will be easily accessible for viewing, printing and sharing from your computer.

Following are eight scans showing the different formats you can save items as. You can easily see here what formats will and will not work for text documents by comparing these. This is ONE scan saved in each format.

These samples are the back of one photo. The words are in Dutch. They are shown alphabetically by format. The views are in Black & White and in Color (sepia tone), although and unfortunately the color views will show as black & white in this book.

The back in a color scan shows pencil writing for the first four lines, blue ink for the next three lines and the photographer studio markings and information is a green-blue shade. Viewing these in color, the BMP is the sharpest view.

All views are the same measurement concerning size. The space each takes in the computer for each <u>color</u> view (larger than black & white) follows:

BMP – 744 KB
JPG/JPEG – 44 KB
PNG – 504 KB
TIFF – 456 KB

Samples follow:

BMP –Preceding is in black & white (unreadable).
You may note a gray shading where the photo is.
Following is in color. Disk space 744 KB.

JPG – Above is in black & white.
Below is in Color. Disk space 44 KB.

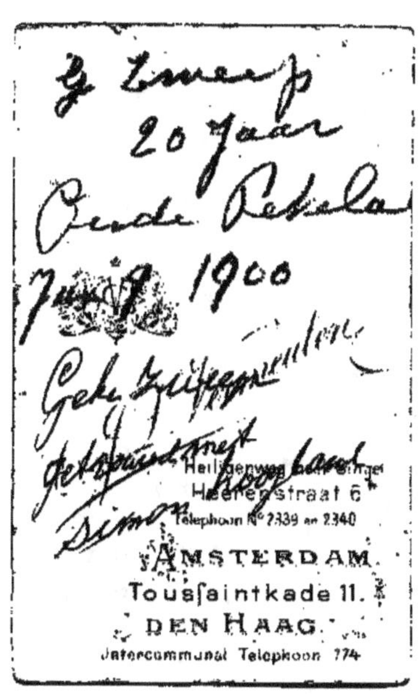

PNG – Above is in black & white.

Below is in color. Disk space 504 KB.

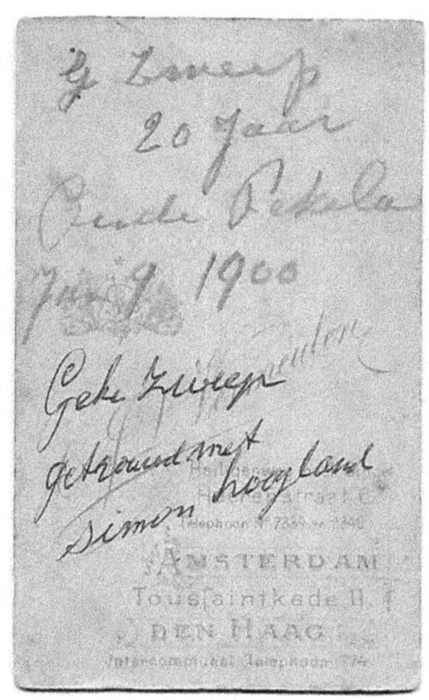

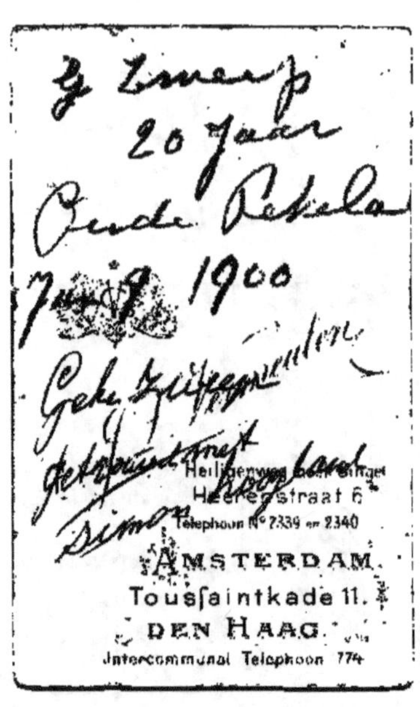

TIFF – Above is in black & white.
Below is in color. Disk space 456 KB.

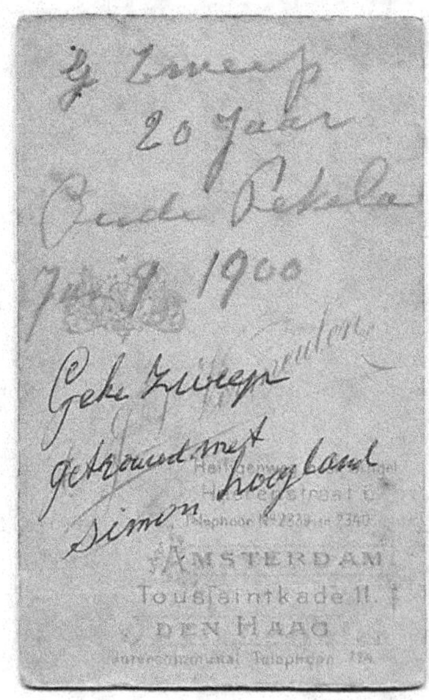

Chapter 7 – Emails with Information

Did you know you can save old emails in other places than your email program?

Did you know that emails are a SOURCE for information you receive? If you receive information from a person, that is a source. What if someone tells you an old family story, where else would you find it?

You will be making another folder at Level #2. You can name it CONTACTS, EMAILS, or any name you want. How is further in this chapter.

For safety sake, and for keeping track of everything someone sent to you or you sent to them that you saved, you <u>do</u> want to preserve those emails.

One way to save those is to copy it to a Word.doc (or similar program), then save it with the date received and pertinent information as Its label. An example: 2010 06 14 (Jun 14) from SMITH Mary 1930-2014. The ending dates reflect when she was born and died for clarification of who the writer is.

The other way, which I also do, is to save the email to at least two folders, depending on what other person or people are mentioned within the email. This involves new subject labels.

I will begin this explanation with a labeling format.

The below is actually very simple but I am putting detailed instructions for this as few know how to do any part of this.

How to label those old emails to make sense is a simple date and name process. You will be storing them elsewhere than in your email program and you will keep your email program 'clean' from older emails. There is nothing worse than to hunt and peck for an ancient email IF you remember 'it' is there.

As you do this and you find those old emails, it is important to understand that the date you receive an email is important. To rename it for filing, as you file it, look first at the date. Let's say you received and sent total of six emails in one day, they being to and from one person. Using this formula, they will file themselves in order. You just have to know where to file them.

Take the date of 'Sat/9/2/2006 5:51 AM' as an example. You will file this as '2006 09 02 0551am' (with no quotes) and add name information such as (example) CARVER to SMITH. That makes your filing label in full as '2006 09 02 0551am CARVER to SMITH'. If the time was pm, just change the 'am' to 'pm'. Note where I have added extra zero's for dates and early times of the day.

You will be saving the emails to TWO folders in your main genealogy computer folder. One is to keep all emails from and to one person in one file. The second is to keep information ABOUT a person in the correct people folders. Save it first to the person you are in contact with and then secondly to the other folder or folders (who is mentioned in the email). Assuming you also have a 'People Folder' for this person, you can save copies there also. This is where I save a copy that has been copied to a Word.doc.

Email Save #1 (the first file for saving email contact letters): The first folder to save your old emails to should be in a folder named 'Genealogy CONTACTS – Family Connections' (no quotes) or a name you choose.

It is in layer #2 of your folders, a 3rd sub-folder at level #2. This folder will keep everything from and to each person and all people you have been in contact with grouped in one area.

- Family Research - PEOPLE
- Genealogy CONTACTS - Family Connections
- Genealogy Overflow

Above is an example of level #2, adding 'Genealogy CONTACTS – Family Connections'.

You now want to make a subfolder IN 'Genealogy CONTACTS - Family Connections' labeled with the contact persons last name and then first name. This is a layer #3, but level #1 within the contacts folder.

Begin the FOLDER label with the word 'email' (no quotes) to help ID what the folder is if you ever do a computer search for something. If the folder name begins with 'email' you know it is an email and not in a People Folder. Following is the 'road map' to the CONTACTS – Family Connections main folder:

Genealogy – ALL HERE >
Genealogy CONTACTS – Family Connections

At times you may receive emails from someone who does not want to give you their last name. It does happen. Examples for folder headings are shown below. You can add further identifiers to labels such as 'SMITH line' or 'From Michigan'.

email Beth yuib@erinet.com (SMITH line)
email CARVER Joan
email JONES Mary
email MOORE Beth
email TAYLOR Ralph

Above, shows level #3 being placed under 'Genealogy CONTACTS – Family Connections'. This is the second level of 'Genealogy CONTACTS – Family Connections'.

You can add to headings to suit yourself, but keep the date and name headings as shown above. The goal is to keep the headings short.

To Clarify:

(1) Open your main genealogy folder.
(2) Make your Genealogy CONTACTS – Family Connections folder (shown on preceding page).
(3) Make a sub-folder in that new CONTACT folder titled 'email xxxNAMExxx' for each person you have been in contact with (not for each email) as shown above for level #3.

Note that it is really hard to add a family name line of research following the label name, as shown for Beth with an email address in the example, as often an email may be about varied family surnames considering the women.

You want to keep all emails FROM or TO a person in one file for each person you have been in contact with.

You may want to save emails from people that were not connected to you. This is a reference that you have been in contact with that person and it stops repetitive communications. If you receive information on a forum or message board, you can save those in a Word.doc and file them into these contact folders, along with copies in any People folder for a family member if any are mentioned.

Email Save #2 - The second file to save to for email contacts and letters: The second folder to save emails to is the PEOPLE file that the email is about, or rather who the information pertains to. This is NOT the person the email is from or to. It is who is being talked about. This is the 'Family Research – PEOPLE' folder files. If the person IS a family member, do save a copy to that persons file.

Of course one email can contain information on more than one person so you can actually save a copy of the first 'save #1' to each person mentioned. This also helps you build your people files in the folder named 'Family Research – PEOPLE'. If you do not have a People file or folder in your computer already made for a person mentioned within an email, make one now.

How to save and file an email into (1) the Contact folder and (2) the PEOPLE FOLDER file:

(1) Go to the original email in your email program and open it.

(2) Click on 'Forward' as if you were going to forward it to someone else.

(3) You will see a small area above the text IN the email body. You CAN add notes into this at this time, or at a later time concerning this email or this person. Examples of notes you may want to add are:

. This person had a wrong family line. Not related.

. This person died in 2004. No further contact info given for her family.

. She sent four photos of her g-grandmother, Joan SMITH, received 2003.

(4) Click on 'File'.

(5) Click on 'Save As'.

(6) Scroll to your main genealogy folder ('Genealogy ALL HERE').

(7) Click on 'Genealogy Contacts' (one of the folders you made at level 2).

(8) Open the contact person name folder (that should have been made prior to doing the save – see level #3 this chapter). This is the person at the other end of the email.

(9) Type in your new 'File Name' (<u>see examples at end of this chapter</u>) IN the 'SUBJECT' line and **DO leave (or re-add) the '.msg' showing at the end**. Then save it. The '.msg' means this opens with your email program. <u>Also</u> save it to any needed People folder.

(10) Close the 'forward' email. (This closed 'forward' may show in your draft or deleted folder. If so, once you are sure it is saved, that extra copy should be deleted.)

(11) Go to the persons email contact folder and make sure the email is there. If you missed a layer, drag it to the correct person in the email Contact folder. Sometimes opening a second window helps with dragging items. Cut and paste also works.

(12) You can now delete out the original email in your email program - OR - if you want, save it (drag it) to a new folder in your email program named to show you have copied it (Emails Family COPIED) with subfolders per contact name.

To SAVE it to WHO the email is about (Save #2) being one or more people, go to the first save (the one you just did) in the contact folder and do a 'copy'. Then go to your People folders and 'paste' it to each person.

Make sure adjustments were done in your new headings (your newly saved email copies) with the names to show who it was to or who it was from. Continue with your next email.

I myself delete emails out of my email program after I do the above two saves. I found that not doing so just builds confusing clutter that is not needed. After a few of these saves, you'll be a professional at it. This is your choice: If you are unsure of what you are doing at this time, save it to a newly named email folder in your email program named to show you have copied contents within it.

Remember that something someone tells you that you did not know is now your documentation, otherwise now known as your source or a source. It may be an old family story that you will not find in any official government record or book. If it came to you in an email, you now have saved that documentation in a findable location. Remember too that the person on you are emailing with should ALSO have a People folder made in your computer if it IS a family member and that person should be entered into your genealogy program. You should also save a copy of all emails to and from that person in that folder.

Following is examples of a few emails shown in a Contact folder named 'email JONES Mary'.

    2004 03 14 0631am JONES to SMITH

    2004 03 14 1100am SMITH to JONES

    2007 11 01 0401am JONES to SMITH

    2007 11 03 1224pm SMITH to JONES

By glancing at the above it tells you that JONES made the first contact, Smith wrote the last email and there was a seven month gap in the limited communications. It also lines up all emails in the correct date format, oldest to newest in this view.

PEOPLE SUMMARIES

A 'summary' is your visual to what you have and what you would like to have concerning a person. You can use it for a variety of reasons, including emailing it to others or print it out and take it on a research trip.

You should now have your paper files organized and scanned to your individual people folders in your computer. All of the computer genealogy items that you had in your computer should now be organized and into those same individual people files also.

Do not be surprised if you later find a random loose document or note item somewhere at home or in the computer as that does happen. Just follow the organization plan.

.....

Pick a person to work on to do your first summary. Enter this person into your genealogy program NOW if you have not done so. Do the Name, Birth Date, Baptism date (if known), Marriage and Death Date if known into your genealogy program. Entering the above at least is organizing and you can work off of your summary later for further information entry if you choose to do so. Remember, women are entered by their birth surname.

.....

A summary is just what it says. It is a summary of a life. These are done in a Word.doc or equivalent program and filed in the persons People folder.

Do not worry about doing summaries for everyone all at once. You will work on these as you want to work on your choice of person.

.....

Each person gets their own summary. You will be looking at everything you have in the People folder for that person. As you work on this DO expect to be doing more research for other people as you work on their summary. You may find that as you are organizing one person's folder that there are things needed and you may be surfing the web for days for things on just that one person.

Keep in mind that documents for another person may refer to this person also. You can easily go to another person's folder, copy the item and paste it to the folder (the person) you are working on. This is where with organizing, that the copy and paste feature comes in.

Begin with who you want to. You can begin with yourself if you want. I recommend starting with someone you have very little information on for learning purposes and you can always add to a summary later.

....

On my main screen using Word Document, I have one Word.doc saved that is labeled '! Summary blank' (no quotes). You can place this within the main Genealogy folder. I type in a name, save to the persons file and close it. I then go to the persons file and open the named document. The name itself should be Last, Middle, First name, year of birth, year of death and possibly a short ID note (example) such as 'was 3rd son named John'. This right away tells me it is the third 'John' child to a married couple.

Following is the blank summary you will make in a Word document. This is where you are going to enter information about a person. You can alter yours. The text that shows in this sample is for easy visuals. Under the '…' is where you can enter anything you need to and it can be hundreds of pages long.

! Summary

Name variations:

...

Father:

Mother:

Siblings:

Spouse:

Children:

SS #:

...

When you start a summary for a person, open this 'Summary BLANK'.

Next to the word 'Summary' ON the 'form' remove the word 'blank'. You will add the last name, first name, birth year and death year. Example: SMITH John 1850-1925. This will be your top line in the persons summary.

Again, save it to the People folder you are working on and change the label (the document label) in that save (Example: ! Summary SMITH John 1850-1925).

Close the original 'blank' word document that you first opened. You do not need to resave it. The blank you just closed will be there for your next person.

Go to the persons file where you just saved that newly named summary. Rename that summary document if need be as some computers will not save the '!' or the dash. Rename the summary to reflect the full title. The '!' use is to keep it at the top of any other word documents that may be added to the file. An example of a finished summary title should show as shows in the previous example.

After filling in those areas shown in the blank summary, save it again and <u>continue adding information</u> for the person now or later, adding in your findings. Be sure to SAVE after entering any new information. I chose to do list events by date. That makes my summaries time lines with facts and visuals added, but you can do it as you prefer.

You can add as much detail as you want to a summary. This is YOUR summary work. Strive to make the summaries complete with all you can find for a person.

To add things to the summary and organize a person's file: Look at what you are holding in this persons folder. Start with one item. Enter it into your summary. DO enter all details for the item. When you are done with that item, do a folder for it within that person's folder if there is not one for that item (like a birth certificate). Begin with a dot (if you are done with the item), space, date of item (year for), last name, first name and what it is.

As you add in the information to your summary from what you have in your computer for that person, do a folder for each item. After you DO have everything possible for that item entered into your summary, rename the item folder by putting a dot in front of that folder name. Example: You have a folder named SMITH John 1875-1951. Within that folder you have subfolders by various names. One named '1895 Military SMITH John 1875-1951' now has all information and visuals entered into your summary. Change the subfolder name to '. 1965 Military SMITH John 1875-1951'. This tells you that you are done with that folder and it will cycle to the top of the list depending on your sort setting. Continue with all 'item' folders for that person.

When you are finished with item folders, rename the PERSON'S folder with the dot and it will cycle to the top. This tells you that you are done with that person concerning information entry with what you have. That persons main folder that holds the subfolders will now be named (example) '. SMITH John 1875-1951'. IF you are sure you can still find more for that person, do NOT rename the person's main folder with that 'dot'.

The dot in front of a file means you have handled that file and are done with it. You can actually work off of your summary for entries into your genealogy program.

An example of a person's folder where all CONTENTS has been added to the summary follows. This is a partial view as information for this person is extensive.

. 1855-1856 Baptism John Jr AMONS

. 1858 Parents married

. 1860 Census AMONS John J [JR]

. 1861 City Dir AMONS John J [SR & JR]

. 1862 City Dir AMONS John J [JR]

. 1863 City Dir AMONS John [JR]

. 1864 City Dir - NO AMONS

. 1865 City Dir - NO AMONS

. 1870 City Dir - NO AMONS

. 1874 City Dir AMONS John J [JR]

. 1874 Military John AMONS JR

. 1875 City Dir AMONS John J [JR]

. 1876 City Dir AMONS John J [JR]

. 1878 City Dir AMONS John J [JR]

. 1880 Census AMONS John J [JR]

. 1882 City Dir AMONS John J [JR]

. 1883 Jul 17 court AMONS John J [JR]

. 1883 Nov 4 Assaulted

. 1884 Shot & City Dir AMONS John J [JR]

. 1886 Accident

. 1886 City Dir AMONS John J [JR]

. 1887 City Dir AMONS John [JR]

. 1887 Marriage AMONS John J [JR] & BLACK..

. 1888 Centennial Exp Cinn

. 1888 City Dir AMONS John J [JR]

. 1893 Cinn city dir AMONS

. 1894 City Dir AMONS

. 1895 City Dir AMONS John J [JR]

. 1896 City Dir AMONS John J [JR].jpg

. 1897 City Dir AMONS John J [JR]

. 1898 City Dir AMONS John J [JR]

. 1898 Daughters death (Birdie E AMONS)

An example of a person's main folder for one person that is DONE and nothing can be added shows the dot or period at the front of the line.

. AMONS John J [JR] 1855-1907

A summary shown on the web, the final work for this person, can be seen at http://stfelixmdflint.blogspot.com/2013/02/amons-john-julius-1855-1907.html All visuals were INSERTED into a Word.doc, not copy and pasted.

The items containing the facts are in his folder. The Word.doc summary that was done for him was copied to the website.

Note: 'Done' does not mean that you cannot add more if more is found for a person.

Later you can add more to your genealogy program if wanted. Just build YOUR routine.

If your summary is totally done, as done as you are willing to work on that person, see if your program allows you to attach your summary in PDF format to that person IN the program or if you can copy it to a 'tag'. It will save you a lot of work. DO save your Word.doc for any changes or additions.

Chapter 9 - Census and Other Visuals

If you would like to add a copy of the original census page or pages to a summary there is an easy way to do it without showing the entire census page. You can show the heading and the family members only.

Download a free 'snipping' or 'snap' program if you do not have one. They seriously only take a few minutes to learn.

With using this tool you can snap views, including doing a crop and save, saving it as a JPG. You can then add JPG's to a word document using the Word insert feature. If you need to do two 'snaps', as with the following census view' and want them to show as one view, do a snap of each area and paste each into a Word Document. The saved size will depend on how large you made your screen for doing the snaps. After both are on your Word document and centered, then copy that as one view with the snap program and save it as one JPG/JPEG. You can always size the JPG down if needed.

Once that is done, you can then INSERT (not copy and paste) it to your final summary, attach it to an email or use it where you need to. Once saved to one person listed, you can always copy and paste that to other people folders that may be listed in that household.

You can adjust the size in two ways. First would be by the size of the copy you do (enlarge or shrink the view prior to your snip) and the other is adjusting the size once it is in your word document using the size feature after you insert it.

A finished view follows that uses two saves, this being from the 1880 census and it was saved to each person shown. This shows the Census header and the people in the household.

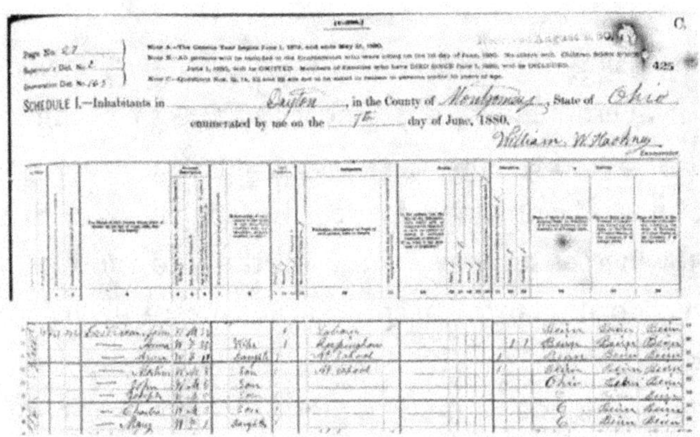

Note that with a census, you can actually have three or four needed views with the previous or next page and some years had extra information for some people.

Following is a crop from an 1861 map using a snap and save program. This was actually saved to nine different people.

The snipping tool comes in handy for a lot of uses when you really need to copy something from one item. Get the view you want and save it in a JPG/JPEG format. It is great for copying and showing old document signatures. You can also enlarge things like this first. Enlarge from your saved scan or JPG, crop to what you want to snip, then snip, and then save it.

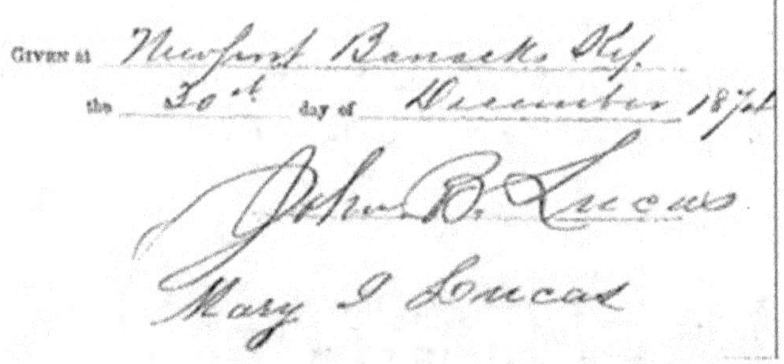

When you save something with a snipping tool, you do want to save it to the person folder it concerns naming it to identify exactly what it is. An example would be the city name, the year, the part of the city. The preceding shown signatures were actually saved to three files, the subject who was the son, the step-father and the mother. One was a save and the other two were a copy and paste.

Two FREE 'snap' programs to snap views are:

http://www.capture-screenshot.org/snipping-tool/

http://www.mirekw.com/winfreeware/mwsnap.html

~ ~ ~

Chapter 10 – Photographs

Do you have photographs that are loose or ones in a variety of albums that you would like to reorganize? Are you in a situation where varied family members all want some or all of the old family photos from childhood and those that exist from earlier time frames? Why not share all with everyone, that including ones the family members have in their possession? You can do so by scanning them.

It is a fantastic idea to put at least key photos of people into your work. You do this by scanning them.

During this past year a cousin to me lost everything in one of the California fires. That included all of the old photographs his parents had from the 1800s and old passports when a family line came to the USA. Thank all good graces that I had borrowed and scanned all of those items some years back! Also lost in that fire were the cremated remains of my aunt and uncle as they were still in plastic containers.

Duplicating photographs is a project to work on after all of your paper and computer treasures are organized and you have your People files made in your computer. Of course, new people files are always going to happen and some new people files may be made due to the photographs you have. Do not forget to add a new person to your genealogy program if they are not added there!

First organize the loose photographs by last names, then by first names, followed by the year or approximate time frame. This helps you match in photos for time periods and even for ones taken on a same day.

While you are working thru your sorting and before you actually start scanning, decide what format you want to save your scans as. When you scan a photograph, you can 'save as' in a variety of formats. Four choices are JPG, TIF, PNG, and GIF. Read up on those. JPG also known as JPEG is not the best quality but many do not want to take up larger computer space with saving things and the quality difference is not noticed by the novice. TIF is your largest file. Details can be found on many varied websites so I won't go into the long details here. For very special photographs you may want to consider saving those in both TIFF and JPG formats.

When scanning, you DO, especially for a JPG, want a high resolution. You do not want excessive but more resolution than what automatically may come up by the program. Your scanner program may tell you that the higher resolution is not needed, but it is wise to ignore that as you want an excellent copy of the original. If you see a white line or blue line in the scan, lower the resolution.

82

Should you decide you want the very best quality and are willing to use up the computer drive space, you should choose a TIF format. I myself use the JPG option for most photograph scans and I scan at a higher resolution than my scanner wants to use. As a test for size differences, scan a photo and save it in all formats. Then check the sizes of each under properties and also visually check for differences. You also may want to print each version to see what the different versions look like in print.

DO – DO – DO OVER scan past the edges of an original photograph. You will use the crop feature in your scanning program for this. Do not forget to scan the backs if ANY information is shown there. Scanning past the edges can often be a great aid with dating a photo and it also gives you a true reproduction of the original photograph.

I keep all photographs scanned in a main photo file to start with. I consider that my main photo file, a safely net, if you will. I have folders each labeled by year. From that file I then copy those to my people files. The largest file is from a wedding anniversary party in the 1930s where I scanned each of about fifty people as crops enlarged plus various sizes of the entire photo. I had to have it scanned at an office supply store as it is so large. From that I was able to do the face crops myself.

<u>FILING your scanned photographs:</u>

Assuming you have no photographs in your computer, start a folder that says 'PHOTOGRAPHS – FAMILY' or any name that works for you. To start, put it on your desktop for ease in finding it when placing photos. If your program wants to open to your My Documents folder after scanning, you can place it there, but then you will spend a lot of time searching to place a scan. Some programs or computers will change to the main folder area no matter where it is after a few scans if that is where you are always heading to, so test that out.

Within your 'PHOTOGRAPHS – FAMILY' folder you will be placing many sub-folders, one for each photo or if many are on one day, it will hold them in that one folder.

NAMING your folder: The ideal option is to start with for an actual photograph is the year or year 'ca' (1900 or 1900 ca), the last name, first name & event in a word or three. Do the best you can but shoot for a year first if at all possible.

An option that I like to use is making the first word 'Photo' as it helps me know what is in that folder in the person folder. It also helps me in various other ways too.   You do NOT need to use capital letters for the word 'PHOTO' as shown.

PHOTO 1880 ca SMITH Mary - Cincinnati OH

PHOTO 1900 SMITH Mary - Anniversary Photo

PHOTO 1905 SMITH Mary - with children

NAMING your photograph: Naming your photograph is usually the same as naming your folder except for adding a little bit of information. Added information would be x100% as original, x400%, face crop x800%, color, b&w, and further as needed. Your computer will add the ending .jpg or whatever your scan is saved as, so do NOT add that on your own. Examples for named photographs follows:

1880 SMITH John Indpls x100% color.jpg

1880 ca SMITH John face crop x800% color.jpg

1880 ca SMITH John face crop x800% b&w.tif

1880 SMITH John waist up crop x300% color.gif

With one photo you can actually end up with many views when you realize how you can bring out detail with cropping to an area of the photo. One example: I have a photo from the very early 1900s of a great grandfather working in front of a tent that has a white spot on it. I scanned that area (crop dcan) at a VERY large size and resolution. It turned out he had a bathtub medallion on the tent. This told me that the magic elixir he made and sold was to put into a bathtub and people were able to bathe at the place (maybe a fair) where he was selling it at that day. What it did not tell me is if he was able to furnish hot water at the tent. If nothing else, it was part of his sales gimmick. Doing scans on two other people shown with him (crops) at the higher settings, I was able to identify who two other people were from matching other photos to them. This was later verified as the correct people by a long lost family member.

Decide if you want to copy your photo and change to a different label for the copy. In that case, copy it, paste it and then rename the copy. Naming a photo can be (examples):

Example #1: 1897 SMITH John at Cincinnati homestead

Example #2: SMITH John 1897 Cincinnati homestead

If you have a few photos taken on the same day, you may have to add an 'a', 'b', or 'c' format or 1, 2, 3 just prior to the '.' (dot). Example: SMITH John 1897 Cincinnati Homestead 1.jpg. If you have ten or more photographs taken on that same day, change the 1 to 01 and so on thru number 9.

You may decide you want the year of birth and death to show with the photo label. In that case, use this format (shown for use for more than one view of the same year and place photo with adding the 1):

1897 SMITH John 1850-1907 at Cincinnati Homestead
1.jpg

For an assumed year, and if your label choice is to list the year first, an assumed year would be entered as '1901 ca'. Example:
1897 ca SMITH John 1850-1907 Cincinnati Homestead
1.jpg

If you are labeling by name first, your 'ca' would show as:
SMITH John 1850-1907 ca 1897 Cincinnati Homestead
1.jpg

Scanning Options:

You may want to scan in varied sizes. FIRST always scan at 100% (full size) and scan the back if anything is on it. This opens the door to doing a folder within that new main photograph folder to keep all together.

Always scan in color and you can also scan in black and white if the original is black and white. You can print a color photo in black and white per printer options BUT you do want an exact duplication. Notes of what you have done can be typed up in a Word Document and saved with the photo in that photo file with the photograph.

Again, on the original first scan, ALWAYS crop to the outer edge so you DO show the entire photo. Again, sometimes the edge can actually help date a photo.

Following are three visuals of what you can do for one photo showing the front and the back. These were cropped from the original scans. The first two are crop views scanned x 100%. The third is a crop view scanned x 800%. Tight crop visuals were done for all four children x 800% but only one is shown here. The front was also scanned a second time x 500%. These are the black and white views of the color (sepia tone) photos showing the aging of the photo, dirt and all.

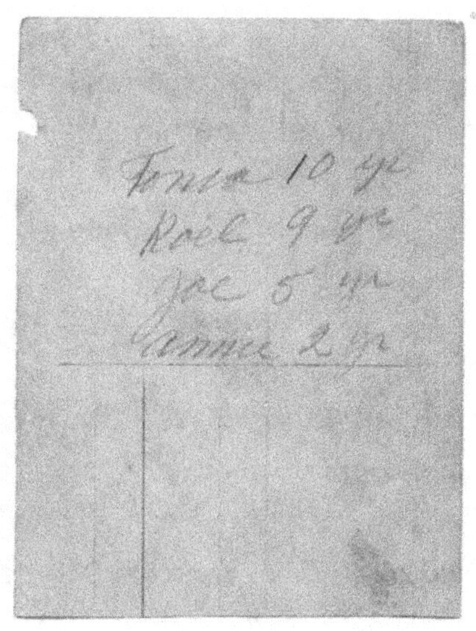

You can see how detail is brought out in this enlarged close view crop of the girl.

Following is an option that can be done that few think about. Have you ever seen a very old photo that has been ruined by hand writing on the original? It is nice they saved the information but .....! You can add words to your scan but NOT ON the photo.

This should be yours second scan. Over scan it a lot at the bottom. This gives you open area off the photograph to add words. Save it. Go back to that 'save' and add words into that open area you just made and resave with adding the word 'words' to that second save label. You will then have three views, one being the original scan scanned just over the photograph edges, secondly an oversized blank word area if needed and the final with words. You will possibly need to do a crop and re-save to remove excess space not used by words. You can add anything you want to within the word area, even the date scanned, scanned by who, and the settings you used. Save your blank ones in case you one day may want to make a change or add information.

 To print something like that you have two choices. Print with the words you have added or crop to the photo and print the photo only. You can size it to what you want. The FIRST scan should be x 100% so it will be true to the actual photograph when printed.

If you decide you want to save anything further from your scans, be sure to change the photo label in some way. Adding a letter or number will do it. If you save a change and do NOT adjust the photo label, you will overwrite that main photograph (you will lose it).

You can save that crop adding 'crop no words' to the label. An added benefit to saving your scan with blank space is that in the future you can change the wording. Rename it before saving to keep your blank copy. NOTE: It is wise to make a copy and then open the copy to add words.

IF a photo is large enough, you can print it with the words and it will print on two papers. Put the word paper on the back side and put it into a front-back clear frame or dual frame.

A powerful free program to add words and more is found at http://www.faststone.org/. It offers many other features for use. REMEMBER when you add words, add the word 'words' to the photo labeled version so you do not alter your original blank word photograph.

Following are two examples of over scanning (scanning way over the edge) to add words, with the words added.

The first is one of those tiny dime store machine photos from the 1930s. This actually has her finger prints on it and it is noted with the photo in the wording. The finger prints were not noticed as being that until the photo was scanned at an enlarged size.

The second is of a color slide that was scanned and is shown here in black and white. The black is actually not part of the original photo. It states when scanned and by who, who owns the photo and other details.

Both are shown here in a much smaller scale than possible due to book size and are too small here for you to read the print.

Anne Christine FLINT
Age 16. 1936
A dime store machine photo cut from the strip and sent to brother, Bill FLINT.
- Enlargement -
Two beige areas are her fingerprints as taken from machine wet.

The following two photos are where extra space was scanned below each photo, then saved with a new name to allow wording and then the wording was added. It is now part of the digital photo but can be printed with the wording not showing by cropping to the photo. Do NOT do a 'save' without a <u>rename</u> if you do crop to print the photo only. You will alter the original digital that shows the wording, that meaning that your new save will now have no words. The added words will be gone.

1909 Mary Elizabeth, aka Maria Anna (QUINN) with husband,
Harry Clarence ST. FELIX, aka FELIX and daughter, Marcella.
This is the only photo of Marcella that exists and also the only
photo with Mary & Harry together. Ufortunately it's not clear.

1953. FOUR GENERATIONS, taken on St. Paul Ave near the corner
of St. Paul Ave & Xenia Ave, Dayton, Ohio. Left to Right:
LeRoy Charles ST. FELIX; William Franklin QUINN;
Anna (GRILLMEIER) QUINN; Mary Elizabeth, aka Maria Anna
(QUINN) ST. FELIX - SEAMAN (& soon to be LEHNERT);
Donna M. ST. FELIX (child). ..... This was the day Mary re-met
Peter LEHNERT, her to be third husband, while the photos were
being taken. That brought her back to Dayton, Ohio which led to
LeRoy moving to Dayton (his home town) after LeRoys wife died.

This is what you do NOT want to do.
Do not put words on the photo to distract.
Add that blank space to add wording.

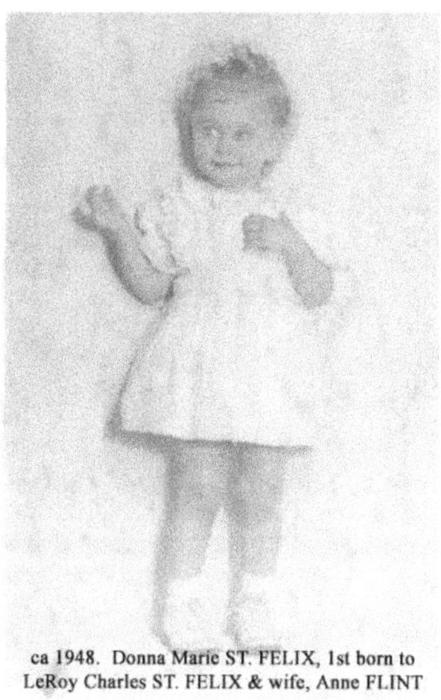

ca 1948. Donna Marie ST. FELIX, 1st born to
LeRoy Charles ST. FELIX & wife, Anne FLINT

These next two photos show a full photo scanned past
the photograph edges to show all of it. The second
view was cropped, enlarged, then had white space
added to the lower edge of the photo in the grass and
wording added.

ca 1943 - Left to Right: Lou KLIPPEL, wife to Fred; Fred QUINN with sister, Mary Elizabeth (QUINN) and Mary's son, LeRoy Charles ST. FELIX, and Fred & Lou's daughter, Lucille. Lucille and LeRoy are 1st cousins.

Following is an example of a photo 'blank'. The blank area for words is in white so it may be hard to see. It is below the light gray line but runs to the ~ mark.

After words are added to a blank, re-crop out excess space from the word area and save with the description to reflect that it has words.

~

The following is a crop view from the previous scan. You can see that with size adjustment when scanning and then cropping, a lot of face detail is shown that does not show in the original.

Reminder: Cropping to print does not affect the original with the words UNLESS you save the new crop OVER the current photo name (you did not change the name) should you have decided to save that new crop. Be sure to change a name when doing a save of a crop of the original. Adding 'crop' or even '2' at the end prior to the .jpg word will work.

Not many people realize that they can also add information to the properties section of a photo after it is scanned. Right click on your view after you have saved it. Go to 'Properties'. Click on 'Details'. Scroll down to 'Comments'. A box will open where you can add a lot of information about the photo. You should be able to see 'Date taken' which is the date you scanned the photo and your name or computer name should automatically be showing. This information cannot be seen by just viewing a photo and definitely not be seen in a printed photo from that scan. The 'date' shown there may change however when you make changes to the properties. Be <u>warned</u> that if you 'Remove Metadata', you wipe out all information in the properties. The text words you add TO the photo, under the photo, will stay.

If you want an index list of photos that you have scanned, you can actually set the 'View' of that new folder to List or a Size of icons. That is a visual index and you can sort per your choice. Do not waste time trying to do a separate list. When you open a folder, any folder anywhere, in case you do not know, can be viewed per your settings. Look above to the word 'View'. Left click. Choose how you want to view those contents. 'Details' will list as a summary.

There are programs that say they can organize your photos for you. What happens if that program does not work with future computers? What happens if you give a copy of your photos to someone and they cannot find anything as they do not have that program? Think ahead and do your labels to make sense to someone 200 years from now.

YOUR SECOND PHOTO SAVE:

As you scan and you are complete with that photo or group of photos in one folder, you want to do a copy and paste of the FOLDER and place a copy in the individual person people folders for that person or people (copy and paste). IF there is more than one person in a photo, do a paste to all individual person folders pertaining to the photo. You will then have the photos in a main photo file showing ALL photographs and a second copy with the person it goes to. Over time, as projects come up, you will be very glad you did this and it is a quick thing to do.

You can do a third save, that being to a folder for just the older photos, all copied to that folder also. This may be handy if you know at times you will mail the views to other people in bulk.

SOMETHING YOU MAY ALSO WANT TO DO:

Let's say you just inherited an old photo album from a grandparent or great-grandparent and for some reason you cannot keep all of the photos. Other people wanting some originals would be one reason why. It would be a good idea to do scan copies of all pages to at least visually keep all of the photos together. This shows photo placement and also allows you to share the pages with others but in scanned format.

First, take a photo of the front and back of the album. You will add it to the album folder.

Start a folder in your normal everyday photograph folder or in the genealogy folder labeled (example) 'Photo Album of SMITH, Joseph' (use applicable name) and add whatever may help you identify the person. Scan the PAGES of the album to this folder in full size (x100%) and possibly also in a larger size, naming each page as you scan in a higher than normal resolution. You may need a long scanner bed to do this. Naming examples:
'SMITH Joseph Album pg1 x100% color'
'SMITH Joseph Album pg1 x400% b&w'

 You can also add a Word.doc into that folder with anything you want to note concerning the album and/or the scans you do.

Be sure to check the backs for any information and scan those too if any detail is there. Name the back as the front was named but end the description with the word 'back'.

TIPS ON STORING ORIGINAL PHOTOGRAPHS:

First, always keep originals in a dark, dry place. Scanning should be the last bright light that photos ever see.

After scanning a photo, here is a safe and easy way to store the originals and it includes protection against scratches.

For your original photographs you will need the following items unless you want to deal with many photograph albums.

1: Cardboard photo boxes or cardboard file index card boxes. Strive for Archival Quality. For larger photos, you want archival quality boxes. Large items of any nature, even old Bibles, should be stored in archival boxes.

2: Plastic sleeves, like fitted plastic bags, the type that baseball cards are set into &/or hard plastic sleeves, also used for baseball cards, all of a size to fit the photo loosely. They come in a variety of sizes and can usually be ordered thru a baseball or hobby shop and also on the web. Make sure what you get is archival quality.

3: Yellow sticky papers.

4: An archival pen. You will not be writing on any original photos but you want something safe for being near a photo.

Write details about the photo on the BACK side of the sticky paper and attach it into the sleeve. Then add your photo putting the back side of the photo towards the sticky.

To file them into the boxes, it is your choice per how you decide to file them. You can do so by year or name. Large tabbed index file cards can also be used to separate years or names.

For reference on what format to save a photograph, following is one photo scanned once and saved in four different formats. They are shown in black & white and color (sepia tone), which will show as shades of gray in this book. You might notice which is the sharper view. They also show why you should always scan in color.

The photographer information is a blue-green shade. ... MORE on how to save information with photographs, along with more samples, can be found in my book titled *'Photographs How to Keep the Details and Story with Any Photo in a Permanent Way without Altering the Original Photograph'*.

BMP Format

A black and white scan is not viewable.

Only a slight shading shows up.

The following is in color. Size on disk: 732 KB.

...

JPG/JPEG Format

PNG Format

TIFF Format

The very old original photographs:

I choose to put my very old originals in protective covers and then into the plastic file tubs placed into the file folder for each person.

If someone wants a copy, I have a 'copy' in my computer summary for the person plus the original scan in the computer file for that person. I can print either of those out without going to the original.

———❈———

Chapter 11 - Down the Road and Optional

The following is down the road, long after you have organized all of your paper, computer and photograph items. Do not let this confuse you now. It is an option for you to keep others updated with what you are doing. It can also 'catch' unknown family with their web searches if put on a blog or website.

.....

Using tags in your genealogy program that you can design or name allows you to know what you have done!

.....

A 'TAG' and what that means: To easily explain it I will do so by an example. You have a person who has a name. The name is a 'tag'. The person has a birthdate and that is a 'tag'. The person has a child and that is a 'tag'. Anything you enter for a person is considered a tag. Some genealogy programs may refer to another word for 'tag'.

If your genealogy program allows you to make a tag (the TMG program does) you want to go to one 'tag' named Note. Duplicate it. Then rename the duplication to '! Summary' without the quote marks.

You will eventually attach or copy and paste your summary to that tag named '! Summary'. The reason for the '!' is so that it is found on top area of the tags used for an individual people without searching for it. That makes adding summaries for a person a lot simpler and at instant glance you can see what you have done by looking at that person's tags used.

I do not recommend adding a summary to a person in the program until you have finished researching the person. If you do attach it, you can replace it. The advantage of this attachment is that the tag shown for a person in the program tells you that you have researched all you can for the person. For a few of my people I actually have a Word Document listing what I would like to find, but the searches have been useless.

Following is from a page I have in my program for a family member and the tags shown are for just what I have found for him. This shows three tags I have made for him on top, all beginning with '!' and I will explain.

Following explains part of what is shown.

(1) ! Tribal pages link (this is a tag): I had been entering things also into free (or paid for more bells and whistles) site on line for family to check what I am doing. (Currently I am redoing that for my family members.) You can later do that by use of a GEDCOM which is limited with what it transfers.

- Family has the web link and it saves me from doing a lot of emails.

- This allows them to let me know what I may be missing and also allows the elderly instant access to see it all.

- When I have entered a person to TribalPages (www.TribalPages.com), I note that direct link for that person as a tag in my TMG program. I enter the link to the TribalPages website page in the memo that will show when I open the tag in my program. This link also shows on #2 below.

(2) ! Blog uploaded (this is a tag): For some people I have an excess of information and a lot of photos that will not fit into the free version of TribalPages noted above. For a few I have very old original passports too. The full summary and all else, that including the passport pages in JPEG format, are uploaded to a blog.

At the blog I reference the page as an overflow to the TribalPages page showing that link. At the TribalPages link I also reference the direct blog to the person showing that link there too.   It is a circle to information, if you will.   My choice for a blog is www.blogspot.com for which at the side bar I have added an index, people reached by link at the blog.

(3) ! Summary (this is a tag): As mentioned above, I have attached my summary to the person in my genealogy program.

This is not quick work but it works for many depending on their needs.

~ ~ ~

Chapter 12 - Sources - Oh My!

Sources are a somewhat confusing thing to work with. There are books written just for explaining them.

Basically a source tells you where you got your information from; the what, the where, when you got it and so on.

If you are familiar with web searches, you most likely have seen sources quoted when you find information. A site like www.familysearch.org will show their source at the bottom of a page.

So what do you list as your source? You got it from a website, right? Well yes, but should you list their source? Actually yes that too.

However, if you do not want to deal with sources at this time as you are expected to do as you are not yet ready to deal with entering sources into a genealogy program, you can at least save the web link, but remember that they can change.

Here are two options:

In an individual persons computer folder, for each item you have for that person (separate folder for each item), you can add a word document for that item and name it (example) '1889 Birth notes Jones Sue'.

Within that 'note' you can list the link you found the item at. At least you can easily get back to it on the web. You can also copy the source information shown there for that item. If it came from a paid membership site it is a good idea to copy that source information while you are there.

An example of a full source shows below.

"United States Social Security Death Index," index, FamilySearch (https://familysearch.org/pal:/MM9.1.1/V9S4-NZQ : accessed 09 Jul 2014), Harry Felix, Dec 1975; citing U.S. Social Security Administration, Death Master File, database (Alexandria, Virginia: National Technical Information Service, ongoing).

You can enter sources into your genealogy program when you are ready to deal with sources. You can also add it to your summary. Word Documents do allow the use of Endnotes and Footnotes.

If you need to read up on sources, it is said your best read on it is titled *Evidence* by Mills.

Very often you will find on the web works done by others. Use that information as leads ONLY, not absolute truth. There is overwhelming errors put out by others, often done by assumptions and not in depth research for proof. Many are just copied from the works of others. The website you found that 'something' would be a source. If you can make contact with a person for it, be sure to do good documentation with what they furnish to you and list them in your contact list.

Chapter 13 – DNA

If you have had a DNA test done, you know you are dealing with a mess of its own. Keep good records in a file for DNA and don't copy anything to a People File unless you have definite proof.

An example of how a DNA test can solve a mystery is within my own family this year.

We have a person five generations back that was thought to be our ancestor; that is until I found that he had died six years prior to a child being born. The child, per the 1850 census record, actually showed twins who had the names of Levi and Mills, neither being the name we knew as a great-grandfather. We had previously figured that one of the twins died and the other was renamed.

I thought on it, kept searching and then I decided to follow a known brother to the father who wasn't, as that was the family name. I found that during that 1850 census, the brother showed no infants in his home but ten years later a child born in 1850 was in his household. I tried to track a birthdate for the child and could only come up with a month and year. Nothing showed a day. The month and the year did match to my 1850 census ancestor. My assumption was that the brother slept with the widow to his brother;

that he was the father of twins, and one was given to him after they were weaned. It was a wild guess and the only way we could possibly be related to that lineage that lineage being the direct surname line for my father.

Then, one of my sisters did a DNA test. After figuring out how it all worked she found someone who descended from that other twin and my assumption turned out to be correct. The connection opened up heritage we couldn't earlier track due to information that person furnished.

I would still like to find proof of the actual day of birth for that other person but nothing, including the 1930s death certificate, states the day. We do have proof though that we descend from the line, just not the way one would consider Hoyle with what is considered normal, moral standards. In my summary for that person, I have in red 'NEED BIRTH DAY'. Both of the twins do show birth in March 1850. Only one shows a birth day with the death certificate.

Chapter 14 - Closing Note

I tried to keep the explanations easy to read and understandable along with being very specific on the previous pages. There is nothing worse for me than to read and read on useless pages just to be overwhelmed with glassy eyes.

I do want to mention that you can adjust your routine as it works for you. It is very important to get all steps in and the previous routine works best to avoid missing steps with saving items, information and documenting.

It is very important to have IN each person's folder everything you have for that person and achieving that is where you MUST be organized.

I have many computer people folders where people have dozens of items sitting there waiting for me to organize the contents. Knowing which is not complete is easy with that '.' (dot) in front of their name on their folder for the finished ones.

Your goal for the computer People Folders is:

(1) All you physically hold, including photographs, is scanned and a copy is in the persons file along with all things found on the web for that person.

(2) Each item is entered into a summary and eventually into the _perfect_ genealogy program.

Taking on the project of family research IS a slow process, but you knew that didn't you. Think of it as mental stimulation (exercise) and make good notes as you think of things you want or need to do!

For those that have used the email lists at Rootsweb.com, you know there is a list (postings) for all types of things from people to places and more. It was bought out by Ancestry.com and has been closed down at length. It is now operational with more coming back almost daily. It is also still FREE. It is a good place to find family ties and information.

For those researching African-American genealogy you might want to check out the books by Alex K. Patterson at Amazon.com. It is a series in progress that I ran across while searching for a northern slave owner. I did find him in book one of the series. The books contain slave and owner names, many with details.

A note from the author

Thank you and I sincerely hope this book helps you. Just remember it takes time to get organized and a good routine is needed for how you do and store things.

If you enjoyed your experience with this book, your favorable feedback to where you purchased the book is very much appreciated.

Current books by D. M. KALTEN

www.amazon.com/author/kalten